CLASSIC W... 'N

TODAY'S ...vERS.

Looking for ....uance for the dilemmas of the spiritual life? Find it in the company of the wise spiritual masters of our Catholic tradition.

Comfort in Hardship: Wisdom from Thérèse of Lisieux

Inner Peace: Wisdom from Jean-Pierre de Caussade

Life's Purpose: Wisdom from John Henry Newman

Path of Holiness: Wisdom from Catherine of Siena

A Simple Life: Wisdom from Jane Frances de Chantal

Solace in Suffering: Wisdom from Thomas à Kempis

Strength in Darkness: Wisdom from John of the Cross

Forthcoming volumes will include wisdom from:
Francis de Sales
James Alberione
Luis Martinez

Solace in Suffering

Solace in Suffering

Wisdom from Thomas à Kempis

Edited and with a Foreword by Mary Lea Hill, FSP

Pauline
BOOKS & MEDIA
Boston

Library of Congress Cataloging-in-Publication Data

Thomas, à Kempis, 1380–1471.
  [Selections. English. 2010]
  Solace in suffering : wisdom from Thomas à Kempis / edited and with
an introduction by Mary Lea Hill. — Classic wisdom collection.
      p. cm.
  ISBN 0-8198-7135-4 (pbk.)
  1. Suffering—Religious aspects—Catholic Church. I. Hill, Mary Lea.
II. Title.
  BX2373.S5T5613 2010
  248.8'6—dc22

                          2010018528

Cover design by Rosana Usselmann

Cover photo by Mary Lou Winters, FSP

Published by Pauline Books & Media, 50 Saint Pauls Avenue, Boston, MA 02130-3491.

Printed in the U.S.A.

www.pauline.org

Pauline Books & Media is the publishing house of the Daughters of St. Paul, an international congregation of women religious serving the Church with the communications media.

1 2 3 4 5 6 7 8 9   14 13 12 11 10

For Sister Joan Mary Ravetto, FSP
who taught us the Imitation of Christ

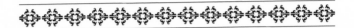

Contents

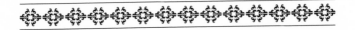

Foreword:
Imitation of Christ—
The Paradox of Suffering

As I am writing this, one of my thumbs and two other fingers are having trouble paying attention to their duties; my knees and their surrounds are entering their third decade of deterioration; my shoulders are rounding, and so forth. We do expect older bodies to break down over time—just not our own bodies. And we genuinely sorrow at the young being burdened by physical or mental sufferings. We live in a world wracked by, and wrapped in, suffering—no matter where you look you see poverty, natural disaster, sickness, persecution, war, and injustice of every kind.

I'm reluctant to admit it, but I've always had a love/hate relationship with suffering. I blame this not on Jesus, but on the saints. If they hadn't made it so blessedly attractive to walk into an arena of lions, or into the wilderness to encounter savage beasts, or to endure intense pain and exhaustion, I could have lived a life happily shunning suffering. However, to this day I have maintained this love/hate relationship with suffering. I loved theirs and hated mine. That needs some clarification. The lives of the saints aren't the problem in themselves; it's the way their biographies have been written. Authors concentrate on the spectacular and sometimes leave a complete vacuum when it comes to the everyday tedium. This is where the beauty of *The Imitation of Christ* comes in. The author, Thomas à Kempis, has drawn a balanced biography of human suffering as it will play out in our own lives, how it can be evaluated and valued in relation to the cross of Christ. *The Imitation* itself reads as a whole rule of life—in fact, it was written for monks—but it can easily be adapted to the life of any serious Christian. Yet as we contemplate these things, we find we need to grapple with two big questions:

1) What is the *paradox* of suffering? Isn't all suffering bad?

2) What does *imitation* of Christ mean? Aren't we expected to know who we are and be ourselves?

To begin with the second question, we may remind ourselves that we *are* Christ through our Baptism. So the process of imitating Christ is really the process of identifying ourselves with him. This transformation is a lifelong work.

In the ancient world, masters gathered disciples around them, disciples who stayed with that master all the time, for the purpose of imitation. Jesus clearly stated, "If any want to become my followers, let them deny themselves and take up their cross and follow me" (Mt 16:24). He also said, "... learn from me; for I am gentle and humble in heart" (Mt 11:29). Following those footsteps implies the cross of suffering. Yet the cross of suffering is not all bad—the cross is the source of the great joy of our salvation.

We sign ourselves with the cross, hang it on our walls, and object when crosses are removed from public places, yet we fear living under the shadow of the cross. How sad and unsavvy! Though we feel wise, we fail to understand an important point: we can't escape the cross. Do you know anyone who has no suffering (disappointment, betrayal, physical or psychological illness, loss to death, depression)? With all that, besides the inner sorrow of not understanding ourselves, failing our own expectations, and so on, why try to slip out from under the shadow of the cross? It seems as though we want to shrink from our greatest love, our best blessing—the benevolent gaze of God.

I once heard of a young boy who was upset and a bit frightened by a wall decoration in his grandmother's house. We've all seen them. It read: "God sees you!" Noticing his discomfort, Grandma explained, "It doesn't mean that God is out to get you, but that he loves you so much that he can't keep his eyes off you." This shadow of the cross, then, is really like a cloak of justification, an assurance of the Lord's protective presence, a guarantee of his love.

To return to our first question, the *paradox:* according to the dictionary, a paradox is something contrary to expectation. That definitely defines suffering as it appears in our lives. We never anxiously await suffering. It comes often unexpectedly and is usually unwelcome. We view it as a puzzle to be solved or a trap to escape from. But the paradox of suffering is in its unexpected benefit—in its *blessing,* in fact.

"Therefore, take up your cross and follow Jesus, and you will attain eternal life" (Book 2, Chapter 12). This is the essential message of *The Imitation of Christ.* It is an ascetic work meant to inspire and prod us in our search for meaning in life, especially in life's mundane and difficult aspects. *The Imitation* is actually four books in one: *Useful Admonitions for a Spiritual Life, Admonitions Concerning Interior Life, Interior Consolation,* and *The Sacrament of the Altar.*

It is commonly believed that Thomas à Kempis was the author, although the book was published anonymously. There is a preserved volume, however, that bears his signature. In any case, *The Imitation* is the product of a school of spirituality that was prevalent throughout the Rhine Valley and the Netherlands in the 1400s. This school is generally referred to as *Devotio Moderna,* the New Devotion. It was a school of reform in its day, an attempt to revitalize the Church by showing how to live a life of simple devotion. So, author or not, through *The Imitation*, Thomas became the spokesman for his times.

Thomas à Kempis was born Thomas Haemerken at Kempen, a town of artisans near Cologne, in 1380. He left home at thirteen to join an older brother at the schools of Deventer, Holland. Soon, however, Thomas entered religious life among the Brothers of the Common Life, a secular confraternity. This group tried to duplicate the life and spirit of the early Jerusalem church, with each member supporting himself, sharing all in common, and living the evangelical counsels of poverty, chastity, and obedience. Thomas was an accomplished copyist. In fact, he produced a four-volume copy of the Bible that is still extant. In time, Thomas transferred to the newly erected monastery of the Canons Regular of Saint Augustine in

Zwolle, Holland. Here he was ordained a priest, then appointed subprior and given the duty of instructing new members. To fulfill this duty he wrote a number of other works, including *Prayers and Meditations on the Life of Christ, The Incarnation and Life of Our Lord, The Founders of the New Devotion, Sermons to the Novices Regular, Counsels on the Spiritual Life,* and *Meeting the Master in the Garden.* After a long life of service to his community and to the poor, Thomas à Kempis died in 1471 and was buried at his monastery. His remains were later transferred to the Church of Saint Michael in Zwolle. The inscription carved on his memorial reads: "To the honor, not the memory, of Thomas à Kempis, whose name endures beyond any monument."

Why are we still so devotedly reading a book written in the fifteenth century? Literally tons of spiritual books have been written since then, so what is the appeal of this old book? How did it happen to become the most requested Christian book, second only to the Bible itself? A classic!

Some today say it is favored only by more conservative-minded Christians. Perhaps this is so, but I would prefer to think of its devotees as those more *serious*-minded, those who want to know how to live their lives in union with Christ, how to make sense of the many sufferings they face. This is the book, we are told, that our beloved Pope John Paul I was reading the evening he died. Blessed Pope John XXIII revealed in his *Journal of a Soul* that *The Imitation* was his preferred reading after the breviary, the missal, and the Bible. Saint Ignatius of Loyola included it as recommended reading in his *Spiritual Exercises*.

Amazingly, *The Imitation of Christ* has spoken to the contemporary situation of people for more than 600 years. This ability to relate to the human heart, wherever and whenever, has made this small volume a classic.

The pieces we have selected for this volume focus on the ways we are invited to follow in the footsteps of our Lord, to find meaning in joining our suffering with his as we prepare for the blessedness of his kingdom.

Is the style too passive for today's Christians, expected to take responsibility for their faith? We are told to bring our faith on the road, if you will, into the workplace, and into social engagements, as well as into charitable and community commitments. As post-Vatican II disciples of the Lord, we know that if we have drawn near to Christ, we cannot help but take on his attitudes and his interests. The more we have absorbed, the more we will exude. The more we have taken in to ourselves of the spirit of Christ, the more we can give of ourselves to others. Perhaps the tone and the sentiments of *The Imitation of Christ* will not be to your liking; perhaps they will not seem to speak to you—but pick it up out of curiosity or simply out of courtesy to the centuries of its devotees. It *will* say something to your soul.

I

The Imitation of Christ and Contempt for All the Foolishness of the World

"Whoever follows me will never walk in darkness" (Jn 8:12). These are the words of Christ, by which we are counseled to imitate his life and way of acting. If we truly want to be enlightened and delivered from all blindness of heart, then let our principal study be meditation on the life of Jesus Christ.

The doctrine of Christ surpasses all the doctrines of the saints; and whoever has the spirit will find a hidden manna in it (see Rev 2:17). But for many it happens that after frequently hearing the Gospel, it has little effect because they do not have the spirit of Christ. Those who would fully and joyfully understand the words of Christ, must study how they can make their whole lives conform to that of Christ.

Of what use is it to argue profoundly about the Trinity if you have no humility and consequently are displeasing to the Trinity? In truth, sublime words do not make one holy and just. However, a virtuous life makes one dear to God. For my part, I would rather feel repentance than be able to define it. If you knew the whole Bible by heart and the sayings of all the philosophers, what would it all profit you without the love and the grace of God? "Vanity of vanities! All is vanity" (Eccl 1:2), except loving God and serving only him. This is the greatest wisdom: to despise the world and to aspire to the kingdom of heaven.

It is vanity, therefore, to seek wealth and to place your trust in it, when it will certainly disappear. It is vanity also to be ambitious for honors and high positions. It is vanity to indulge the desires of the flesh, and to involve yourself in things for which you will later be grievously punished. It is vanity to wish for a long life and not to be concerned with leading a good life. It is vanity also to be attentive only to this present life, and not to look forward to those things which are to come. It is vanity to love that which passes quickly, and not to concentrate on eternal joy.

Remember often the proverb: "The eye is not satisfied with seeing, or the ear filled with hearing" (Eccl 1:8).

Consider how to turn your heart from what is seen to what is unseen, for those who follow only their senses tarnish their conscience and lose the grace of God.

— From Book 1, Chapter 1 (nos. 1–5)

II

On the Usefulness of Adversity

It is good for us sometimes to have troubles and adversities, for they cause us to look within and recognize that we too are exiles, whose hopes should not be centered on anything in this world. It is good that we sometimes suffer contradictions and that others have the wrong opinion of us, even when our intentions are good. These things are helpful to our humility. They keep us from becoming proud. Because of them we will seek God to witness to our conscience, since outwardly we are despised and not believed.

Therefore one should be so established in God that one has no need to seek many human consolations. When a person of good will is troubled or tempted or afflicted with evil thoughts, that person is better able to understand the need for God without whom no good can be done (see Jn 15:5). Often we complain and sigh and pray because of the miseries we suffer. We become weary of living longer; and wish for death in order to "depart and be with Christ" (Phil 1:23). Our thought is that perfect security and full peace cannot be found in this world.

— From Book 1, Chapter 12 (nos. 1–2)

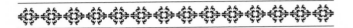

III

On Resisting Temptations

As long as we live in this world we cannot be without tribulation and temptation. It is written that "human beings have a hard service on earth" (Job 7:1). Everyone needs to be aware of temptations and to be attentive in prayer, because "Like a roaring lion your adversary the devil prowls around, looking for someone to devour" (1 Pet 5:8). No one is so perfect and holy as to never have temptations; nor can we be completely without them.

Temptations are often very profitable to us, even though they can be troubling and painful; for in them we are humbled, purified, and instructed. All the saints have lived through many tribulations and temptations and have profited by them. On the other hand, those who could not resist temptation have become sinners and have fallen away. No religious house is so holy, nor is any place so secluded as to be without temptations and trials.

As long as we live we can never be entirely free from temptation because we have within us the source, since we were born with a tendency toward sin. When one temptation or tribulation is over, another arises. We will always have something to suffer because we have lost the good of our original happiness. Many seek to flee temptations and fall more grievously into them. By flight alone we cannot win. However, by patience and true humility we become stronger than all our enemies.

Those who only flee temptations outwardly and do not pluck out the root will make little progress. Instead temptations will soon return and their condition will be worse than before. Patiently, by degrees and with long-suffering you will, with God's grace, overcome them better than by harsh measures of your own making. Seek counsel when facing temptation and deal gently with one who is tempted. Offer the same understanding you would hope to receive yourself.

All temptations begin with meager confidence in God and a scattered mind. Just as a ship without a rudder is tossed around by the sea, so a person who is weak and makes no effort to resist is tempted in many ways. Fire tries iron and temptation tries a just person. Often we don't know what we are capable of doing, but temptation helps us test our mettle. We must be attentive, especially when temptation begins, because then the enemy is more easily overcome. He must not be allowed within at all, but should be resisted at his first knock and kept outside. Someone once advised: "Stay strong from the outset because an illness will be worse if the cure is delayed too long." First a simple thought comes to mind, then a strong image, then delight, evil attraction, and finally, consent. If he is not resisted from the beginning, the wicked enemy gains full entrance little by little. The longer we are negligent in resisting, the weaker we become and the stronger the enemy grows against us.

Some suffer serious temptations in the beginning of their conversion and others at the end. Some are greatly troubled their whole lifetime. Some, in the wisdom of God, seem hardly to be tempted at all. God weighs the state and merits of each one and arranges everything in view of the salvation of the chosen.

So we must not despair when we are tempted, but pray to God even more fervently, asking him to save us from all tribulations. According to the saying of Saint Paul, God, with the testing, "will provide the way out so that you may be able to endure it" (1 Cor 10:13). Therefore, let us humble ourselves under God's hand in all temptations because without a doubt, he will save us and raise us up.

Our progress is proved in temptations and tribulations, and during them there is greater merit, as well as opportunity for our virtue to shine. It is hardly exceptional to be prayerful and fervent when we have no trouble, but we make progress when we patiently endure adversity. Sometimes, although spared great temptations, we are often overcome in little daily ones. Being humbled in this way, we will never presume on our own strength in great things, knowing how weak we are in small things.

— From Book 1, Chapter 13 (nos. 1–8)

— NEVER "GOOD ENOUGH"
— DON'T MATTER TO ANYONE BECAUSE I'M "JUST ONE OF MANY" SO WHO CARES?
— TOO SENTIMENTAL = USELESS
— NOT ACTIVELY INVOLVED SO NOT EFFECTIVE AS A CHILD OF GOD
— HAVE TO LOOK GOOD TO HAVE ANY CREDENCE OR VALUE
— SO DISTRACTED TOO EASILY
— SO SELF-CENTERED — AFRAID OF CONTACT WITH THOSE I DON'T KNOW "

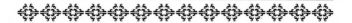

IV

On Interior Conversation

Why are you standing here looking all around? This is not your resting place. "Our citizenship is in heaven" (Phil 3:20), and we should view everything on earth as passing. "All those things have vanished like a shadow" (Wis 5:9), and so will you, too, along with them. Do not cling to them or you may be ensnared and perish. Keep your thoughts on the Most High, and direct your prayer to Christ without ceasing. If you don't know how to meditate on high and heavenly things, dwell on the Passion of Christ, and willingly hide in his sacred wounds. If you focus devoutly on Christ's wounds and his saving scars, you will have great consolation in tribulation. Being despised by others will not shake you, and you will be at ease before your detractors.

Christ was despised by people in this world. In his greatest need he was forsaken by his acquaintances and friends in the midst of insults. Christ was willing to suffer and to be despised—how do you dare complain of anything? Christ had enemies and detractors—do you expect everyone to be your friends and benefactors? How will your patience be rewarded if you have no adversity? If you cannot endure contradiction, how can you claim to be a friend of Christ? "If we endure, we will also reign with him" (2 Tim 2:12).

If you could just once enter perfectly into Jesus' heart and experience a little of his ardent love, then you would not be so concerned about your own convenience or inconvenience. Instead you would rejoice when confronted, because the love of Jesus makes a person forget self. A lover of Jesus and of the truth, a truly interior person, free from inordinate affections, can turn to God, transcend self, and enjoy a delightful rest.

— From Book 2, Chapter 1 (nos. 4–6)

V

On Humble Submission

Pay no attention to who may be for you or against you, but take care that God may be with you in everything you do. Have a good conscience, and God will surely defend you. No malice can hurt the one whom God helps. If you only know how to hold your peace and to endure, you will surely experience the Lord's help. He knows the time and the way you will be delivered, so resign yourself into his hands. It is up to God to help us and deliver us from all turmoil. In order to keep us humble, it is often helpful for others to know our faults and reprimand us.

When we humble ourselves for our faults, we can smooth things over, and easily satisfy those who are angry.

God protects and delivers the humble. He loves and comforts the humble and draws near to them. God bestows grace on the humble, and after they have been brought low, he raises them up to glory. To the humble he reveals his secrets and sweetly draws and invites them to himself. In the midst of reproach, the humble remain in great peace; for they depend on God and not on the world. Never think that you have made any progress until you consider yourself to be the least of all.

— From Book 2, Chapter 2 (nos. 1–2)

VI

On the Good and Peaceable Person

First keep yourself in peace, then you will be able to bring others to peace. The peaceable person does more good than one who is highly educated. The overly passionate person turns even good to evil, and readily believes evil. The good and peaceable person turns all things to good. Whoever is in perfect peace suspects no one. But whoever is discontented and disturbed is agitated by various suspicions, and neither has rest, nor permits others to rest. Often such a person says what should not be said and does not do what should be done. While considering what others ought to do, do not neglect what you yourself are bound to do. It is better to have zeal toward yourself in the first place, and then you may justly exercise zeal toward your neighbor.

You know well how to excuse and gloss over your own deeds, but you will not accept the excuses of others. It is more just for you to accuse yourself and to excuse another. If you wish others to put up with you, then know how to put up with them. See how far you still are from true charity and humility, which does not know how to feel anger or indignation against anyone but oneself. It is easy to converse with the good and the gentle, for this comes naturally to all. And all persons prefer to live in peace with those who agree with them and love them the best. But to know how to live peacefully with those who are stubborn and difficult, or undisciplined and opposed to us, is a great grace. It is worthy of much praise and is a sign of great strength.

Some people know how to live in peace and also enjoy peace with others. Others not only have no peace themselves, but they also do not allow others to enjoy peace. Such persons are troublesome to others, but still more troublesome to themselves. Still others keep themselves in peace and work to restore peace to others. Nevertheless all our peace, in this burdensome life, must be placed more in humble suffering than in not feeling the things that go against our nature. Those who know how to suffer will enjoy much peace and conquer themselves. They will be the lords of the world, friends of Christ, and heirs of heaven.

— From Book 2, Chapter 3 (nos. 1–3)

VII

On the Few Who Love
the Cross of Jesus

Jesus now has many lovers of his heavenly kingdom, but few who bear his cross. He has many who desire consolations, but few who desire tribulation. He finds many companions at table, but few in fasting. All desire to rejoice with him, but few are willing to suffer something for him and with him. Many follow Jesus to the breaking of bread, but few follow him to the drinking of the chalice of his passion. Many venerate his miracles, but few follow him in the humiliation of the cross. Many love Jesus as long as they do not meet with any adversity. Many praise him and bless him as long as they receive consolation from him.

But if Jesus hides himself and abandons them for a little while, they either complain or fall into extreme discouragement.

But those who love Jesus for Jesus' sake, not for any consolation of their own, bless him in every tribulation and anguish of heart as in the greatest consolation. And even if he never gave them his consolation, they would still always praise him and always want to thank him.

Oh, how powerful is the love of Jesus when it is pure and not mixed with any self-interest or other love. Shouldn't those who are always seeking consolation be called mercenaries? Don't they show that they are more lovers of themselves than of Christ, if they are always thinking of their own comfort and gain? Where will we find someone who is willing to serve God gratuitously?

Rarely do we find a person so spiritual as to be devoid of all things. Who can find the person who is truly poor in spirit and detached from the love of all created things? Such a person is "far more precious than jewels" (Prov 31:10). If you were to distribute everything you own, it would still be nothing. And even if you were to do great penance, it would still be a little thing. And if you were to learn all knowledge, you would still be far away. And if you had great virtue and a very fervent devotion, much would still be lacking, that is, the one thing which is supremely necessary. And what is it? After having left all things, you also leave yourself completely and retain nothing of self-love. And when you have done everything that you thought should be done, believe that you have done nothing.

Do not give much weight to what may be considered great, but in truth confess yourself to be a useless servant; as Truth himself has said: "When you have done all that you were ordered to do, say, 'We are worthless slaves; we have done only what we ought to have done!'" (Lk 17:10)

— From Book 2, Chapter 11 (nos. 1–5)

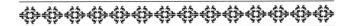

VIII

The Royal Road of the Holy Cross

To many this seems a hard saying: "Jesus told his disciples, 'If any want to become my followers, let them deny themselves and take up their cross and follow me'" (Mt 16:24). But it will be much harder to hear that last word: "Depart from me into the eternal fire" (Mt 25:41). Those, however, who at present willingly hear and follow the precept of the cross will not then be afraid of hearing the sentence of eternal damnation. This sign of the cross will appear in heaven when the Lord will come to judge us. Then all the servants of the cross, who in life have conformed themselves to the crucified Jesus, shall approach Christ their Judge with great confidence.

Why then are you afraid to take up that cross, which leads to the kingdom? In the cross there is salvation; in the cross there is life; in the cross there is protection from your enemies; in the cross there is infusion of heavenly sweetness; in the cross there is strength of mind; in the cross there is spiritual joy; in the cross there is the fullness of virtue; in the cross there is the perfection of sanctity. There is no health for the soul or hope of eternal life except in the cross. Therefore, take up your cross and follow Jesus, and you will attain eternal life. He has preceded you carrying his cross. He died for you upon the cross so that you may also bear your cross and desire to die on the cross. "If we have died with Christ, we believe that we will also live with him" (Rom 6:8). If we are his companions in suffering we shall also be partakers in his glory.

And so all is reduced to the cross, and all consists in dying on it. There is no road that leads to life and to true interior peace except the holy road of the cross and of daily self-denial. Go where you wish and seek as much as you wish; you will not find a more sublime road above, nor a safer way below, than the road of the holy cross. Arrange everything as you please, as it seems best to you, but you will always find something you will have to suffer, either willingly or unwillingly. You will always find the cross. For you will either feel pain in your body, or have to endure some spiritual difficulty in your soul.

Often you will be abandoned by God, often you will be troubled by your neighbor, and what is more, you will often be a burden to yourself. Neither will you find any remedy or comfort which can free you or relieve you, but you must bear with it as long as God wills. For if God wants you to learn to suffer tribulation without comfort, it is so that you may surrender yourself entirely to him and so become more humble through tribulation. No one feels the passion of Christ more intimately than one who has suffered as he did. The cross, then, is always ready and waits for you in every place. You cannot escape it wherever you run. For wherever you go you carry yourself with you, and you will always find yourself. Look up or look down; look out or look in; and in all directions you will find the cross. And so, it is necessary for you to be patient everywhere, if you wish to have interior peace and merit the eternal crown.

If you bear the cross willingly, it will bear you and lead you to the desired end, to that place where suffering will end, a place impossible to find here on earth. If you bear it unwillingly, you make it a heavier burden for yourself, while you still have to bear it. If you fling away one cross, you will certainly find another, perhaps heavier, one.

Do you think to escape that which no one can ever escape? What saint was there without crosses and tribulations in this world? Our Lord Jesus Christ himself was not without suffering even for one hour of his life: "Thus it is written, that the Messiah is to suffer and to rise from the dead on the third day" (Lk 24:46), and so enter into his glory. Why do you seek a way other than this royal road, the road of the holy cross?

The whole life of Christ was a cross and martyrdom, and you seek rest and happiness? You are wrong, so wrong, if you seek anything other than to suffer tribulations, because this earthly life is full of miseries and riddled with crosses. The more a person progresses spiritually, the heavier the crosses are to bear, because the pain of exile increases in proportion to love....

As for consolations, let God give them as it pleases him. On your part prepare yourself to bear tribulations and consider them as the greatest consolations. For the sufferings of this life are not worthy of the glory to come, even if you were to suffer all of them by yourself.

When you have become convinced that tribulation is sweet and, for the love of Christ, pleasing to you, then realize that you are in a good place, for you have found paradise on earth. As long as you cannot bear suffering and you seek to avoid it, all will go wrong with you and tribulation will follow you wherever you go.

If you resign yourself to what has to be, that is suffering and death, things will immediately become better, and you will find peace. Even though you were taken up to the third heaven as was Saint Paul, you would not because of this be guaranteed no suffering. Jesus said, "I myself will show him how much he must suffer for the sake of my name" (Acts 9:16). Therefore, suffering awaits you if you wish to love Jesus and serve him always.

Would to God you were worthy to suffer something for the name of Jesus! What great glory would be yours, how much joy would come to all God's saints, and what an example it would be for your neighbor! Everyone recommends patience, but few want to suffer. Meanwhile you should willingly suffer a little for Christ, considering how greatly many suffer for the world.

Keep firmly in mind that it is good to always live as though you were about to die. The more you die to yourself the more you begin to live in God.

None of us will be able to comprehend heavenly things unless we willingly bear adversities for love of Christ. Nothing is more pleasing to God, and nothing is more salutary for you in this world, than to willingly suffer adversities for Christ. If you were free to choose, your preference should be to suffer adversities for Christ rather than to be comforted by many consolations, because this suffering would make you more like Christ and more similar to the saints. Our merit and our progress do not consist in having many sweet consolations, but rather in tolerating great calamities and great tribulations.

If anything was more useful for our salvation than suffering, Christ would certainly have taught it to us by word and example. He clearly exhorts his followers to bear the cross, saying: "If any want to become my followers, let them deny themselves and take up their cross and follow me" (Mk 8:34). After having read and meditated on all these things, let the conclusion be, that "it is through many persecutions that we must enter the kingdom of God" (Acts 14:22).

— From Book 2, Chapter 12 (nos. 1–7, 10–15)

IX

The Wonderful Effects of God's Love

Disciple

You are "my glory" (Ps 3:3) and "the joy of my heart" (Ps 119:111). You are my hope and "a refuge in the day of my distress" (Ps 59:16).

I need to be comforted and consoled by you because my love is so weak and my virtue so imperfect. Come to me often to teach me your holy way. Deliver me from unruly passions and cure my heart of all disordered affections, so that healed and purified interiorly, I may be able to love with constancy, despite my suffering.

Christc

Love is a great thing, in fact, the greatest of all, because it lightens every burden and bears every misfortune. It carries burdens without feeling them, and makes even bitterness sweet. This noble love of Jesus spurs us on to great things and moves us to always desire the most perfect. Love always wants to desire the highest goods, and does not want to seek out anything base. Love wants to be free, not tied down to affection for this world, so that its burning desire may not be hindered, entangled by luxury, or lessened by any discomfort. Nothing is sweeter than love, nothing stronger, nothing higher, nothing more sublime, nothing more expansive, nothing more joyful, nothing more abundant, nothing more pleasing in heaven or on earth, because love is born from God, and it rests not in created things, but only in God.

One who loves flies, runs, rejoices, and is free, restrained by nothing. The lover gives all for all, and possesses all in all, because he rests in the one highest over all, that sovereign Good from whom all good proceeds and flows. Rather than getting lost in the gifts, the one who loves regards only the Giver. Love knows no measure, but burns with desire.

Love is not burdened by labors, thinks its efforts are nothing, and would like to do even more than it can. It makes no excuses, does not consider anything impossible, but believes that it can do all good things. It is ready to do anything, and it performs many deeds that would cause those who love less to faint and give up.

Love is always alert, even while sleeping. When tired it does not show fatigue; when pressed it is not constrained; when threatened it is not disturbed. But like a lively flame and a burning torch, it rises up and securely overcomes all opposition. The lover knows what to say. The soul's ardent affection cries out to God: "My beloved is mine and I am his" (Song 2:16).

Disciple

PRAYER TO IMPLORE THE GRACE OF GOD'S LOVE

"Let me sing for my beloved my love-song" (Isa 5:1). Let me follow you to the very heights, my Beloved. Let my soul lose itself in your praises, exulting in your love. Let me love you more than myself, and love myself only for you, and, as your law of love commands, may I love all those who love you.

Love is prompt, sincere, devout, joyous, and alive; strong, patient, faithful, prudent, long-suffering, courageous, and humble. When a person seeks self, that person no longer loves. Love is cautious, humble, and upright, not weak, careless, or vain. Love is sober, chaste, firm, quiet, and holds the senses in check.

Love is respectful and obedient to superiors, while lowly and humble in its own eyes. Remembering that one does not live in love without suffering, it is devout and grateful toward God, for it trusts and hopes even when God remains hidden.

Whoever is not ready to suffer all things and stand willingly before the Beloved, is not worthy to be called a lover. One who loves must wholeheartedly embrace all that is hard and bitter for the sake of the Beloved, and never be separated from him on account of painful events.

— From Book 3, Chapter 5 (nos. 1–8)

X

We Should Place All Our Cares in God

Christ

My child, let me do with you what I will; I know what is best for you. You think and judge as human affection moves you.

Disciple

Lord, what you say is true; your concern for me is greater than any care I have for myself. For whoever does not cast all the cares of life on you, stands in great risk (see 1 Pet 5:7). Lord, while my will remains firmly attached to you, do with me whatever you please. Whatever you do with me can only be good. May you be blessed if you want me in darkness and equally blessed if you want me in light. May you be blessed if you wish to console me, and if you wish me to be afflicted, may you always be blessed.

Christ

My child, this is how you must be if you wish to walk with me. You must be as ready to suffer as to rejoice. You must as willingly love to be poor and needy as to be rich and prosperous.

Disciple

Lord, I will suffer willingly for your love no matter what you permit to happen to me. I want to receive from your hands without any distinction the good and the evil, the sweet and the bitter, the joyful and the sorrowful, and to thank you for all that happens to me. Preserve me from all sin, and I will fear neither death nor hell. As long as you do not cast me off forever, nor blot me out of the Book of Life; all the tribulations that will befall me will not harm me.

— From Book 3, Chapter 17 (nos. 1–4)

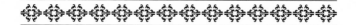

XI

How to Bear
Temporal Miseries with Patience,
Imitating the Example of Jesus Christ

Christ

My child, I came down from heaven to save you. I took your miseries upon myself not out of necessity, but out of charity, so that you would learn how to patiently bear earthly trials without complaint. From the hour of my birth until my death on the cross, I was never without suffering. I experienced great poverty; I often had complaints hurled against me; I patiently bore with confusion and reproach; I received ingratitude for everything I gave, blasphemies for my miracles, and reproach for my teachings.

Disciple

Lord, because in your lifetime you patiently fulfilled the commands of your Father, it is only right that I, sinner that I am, should live patiently according to your will; and as long as it pleases you, bear the burden of this corruptible life for my salvation. Although this present life is burdensome, by your grace it has become very meritorious. As I follow your example and that of your saints, it seems clearer and more bearable despite my weakness.

It is also more consoling than it was before you came, when the gate of heaven remained closed and the way to it seemed darker, and so few concerned themselves with seeking the kingdom of heaven. Then not even the just could be saved or enter into your heavenly kingdom until you suffered and died for the expiation of sin. How much gratitude I owe you for showing me and all the faithful the right and just way to your eternal kingdom. Your life is our way, and by means of a holy patience we walk to you, who are our crown.

If you had not preceded and taught us, who would care to follow you? Alas, how many would remain far behind you if they did not see your splendid example?

Although we are still tepid even after having heard of your miracles and your teachings, what would happen if we did not have so much light to follow you?

— From Book 3, Chapter 18 (nos. 1–2)

XII

On Supporting Injuries
as a Sign of True Patience

Christ

What are you saying, my child? Instead of complaining, consider my passion and the sufferings of the saints. "In your struggle against sin you have not yet resisted to the point of shedding your blood" (Heb 12:4). What you suffer is little in comparison to those who suffered so much, who were strongly tempted, grievously afflicted, tried and tested in many ways.

Therefore, you must recall the gravity of the tribulations that others have suffered, so that you may more easily bear your own small miseries. And if they do not seem small to you, make sure that your judgment does not stem from your impatience. But whether they are small or great, try to bear them with patience.

The better you dispose yourself to suffer, the more wisely you will act, and you will have greater merit. If your mind has been prepared for it and has become accustomed to it, you will find it easier to suffer. Do not say: "I cannot tolerate these things from this person. I shouldn't have to suffer these things, because he has done me great harm and has reproached me for things I never thought of doing. I will suffer willingly, however, at the hands of another, and in the manner that I shall deem best." Such thoughts are foolish because they do not consider the virtue of patience, nor the One who will bestow the crown. Rather, they consider only that person and the offense that has been given.

You are not truly patient if you want to suffer only so much, and only from those you choose. A truly patient person does not mind who does the testing, whether that person excels over you, is your peer, or is subordinate: whether a good and holy person, or someone wayward and unworthy. One who is patient will be indifferent toward the source of the adversity, receiving all with gratitude from the hands of God, and with a positive outlook.

Nothing, no matter how small, if suffered for God, will go unrewarded.

Therefore, be prepared to fight if you want to gain the victory, for "no one is crowned without competing according to the rules" (2 Tim 2:5). So if you do not want to suffer, you are refusing to be crowned. If, however, you desire to be crowned, fight bravely and endure with patience. Without labor one cannot rest. Without fighting one cannot be victorious.

Disciple

Lord, may your grace make possible to me what seems, by nature, impossible. You know how little I can suffer and how quickly I am discouraged by a small difficulty. For your name's sake, help me find all trials lovable and desirable, knowing that to suffer affliction for your love is very good for my soul.

— From Book 3, Chapter 19 (nos. 1–5)

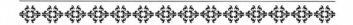

XIII

On Our Own Weakness
and the Miseries of This Life

Disciple

"I will confess my transgressions to the LORD" (Ps 32:5). I confess to you my weakness, Lord. Often what depresses and troubles me is a small thing. I make a resolution to act with fortitude, but as soon as a small temptation comes, I grow anxious. Usually something insignificant causes temptation. And when I think I am fairly safe, I suddenly find myself all but defeated by a light breeze.

And so, Lord, my littleness and my frailty are evident on every side. Have pity on me and "rescue me from sinking in the mire" (Ps 69:14), from being roundly defeated. What often afflicts and confounds me in your presence is this: I am so inclined to fall and so weak in resisting my passions. Although I do not fully consent to them, still, their persistence troubles and grieves me. It is annoying to live in constant conflict. My weakness is so evident to me because my wicked thoughts that rush in wildly never seem to leave.

How I wish that you, almighty God of Israel, ardent lover of the faithful, would see my effort and my sorrow and come to my assistance. Strengthen me with heavenly help, so that my old self, my weak flesh, which is not fully subject to the spirit, which we struggle with our whole life long, may not prevail and dominate.

Alas! What kind of life is this, that has nothing but afflictions and miseries; snares and enemies everywhere? As soon as one trial or temptation ends, another comes. In fact, while the first battle is still going on, others unexpectedly begin.

How can a life, which has such great bitterness, which is subject to so many calamities and miseries, be loved? How can it be called life while it generates so many deaths and plagues? Yet this life is loved, and many take delight in it.

Many say that the world is deceitful and false, yet they do not willingly cast it aside because they are so dominated by the pleasures of the flesh. Some things do make us love the world, while others lead us to despise it. "The desire of the flesh, the desire of the eyes, the pride in riches" (1 Jn 2:16), all these urge us to love the world. But the pains and miseries, which understandably follow these things, breed hatred and disgust for the world.

Know that evil pleasure wins the mind of the worldly soul, who considers it delightful to be given over to the senses. This soul neither sees nor tastes the sweetness of God, nor understands the inner beauty of virtue.

Those who despise the world and make a study of how to live God's holy discipline experience the divine sweetness, which is promised to those who truly renounce all. They can see with greater clarity how badly mistaken the world is and in how many ways it is deceived.

— From Book 3, Chapter 20 (nos. 1–5)

XIV

Finding Rest in God
Above All Good Gifts

Disciple

My soul, above all things and in all things, always rests in the Lord because he is the eternal repose of the saints.

Grant me, most sweet and loving Jesus, to rest in you above every creature—above all health and beauty, above all glory and honor, above all power and dignity, above all knowledge and subtlety, above all riches and arts, above all happiness and exultation, above all fame and praise, above all sweetness and consolation, above all hope and promise, above all merit and desire, above all gifts and graces that you can give and infuse, above all the joy and gladness that the mind can understand and feel, and lastly, above angels and archangels, and all the hosts of heaven, above all things visible and invisible, and above all that is not you, my God!

For you, my Lord and God, are the best above all things—you alone the most high, you alone the most powerful, you alone sufficient, you alone most sweet and most delightful, you alone most beautiful and most loving, you alone the most noble and the most glorious above all things, in whom are perfectly gathered all goods that ever were or ever could be.

Therefore, whatever you give me, other than yourself, or whatever you reveal or promise to me concerning yourself, is little and insufficient, unless I see you and fully possess you. My heart cannot truly rest, or be entirely contented, if it does not rise above all your gifts and all other creatures to rest in you alone.

My beloved Spouse, Jesus Christ, most pure Lover, Lord of all creatures, who will give me the wings of true liberty, to fly and rest in you? When will it be given to me to attend fully to considering how sweet you are, O Lord my God?

When will I be conscious of myself only in you, so that for love of you, I will forget myself and my ways of judging and valuing things, and in a way not familiar to many, be able to lose myself in you alone?

Now I frequently groan and in sorrow bear my unhappiness because in this valley of miseries, I encounter many evils which disturb me, afflict me, and cast a cloud over me. Often they hinder and distract me, allure and entangle me, so that I cannot freely come to you nor enjoy your sweet embraces, which are always available to those you bless. Let my earthly sighs and sufferings move you to pity.

O Jesus! Splendor of eternal glory, comfort of the pilgrim soul! My mouth remains silent in your presence, but my very silence speaks to you.

How long will my Lord delay in coming? Let him come to me, his poor servant, and make me happy. Let him stretch forth his hand and save my poor soul from all afflictions.

Come, come, because without you neither my days nor my hours can ever be happy; for you are my joy and without you my table is deserted. I am miserable, like a prisoner in chains, completely restrained until you comfort me with the light of your presence and restore my liberty by the revelation of your face.

Instead of you, let others seek whatever pleases them. Nothing else pleases me, however, or could ever please me, except you, my God, my hope, my eternal salvation. I will not be silent, nor will I cease to pray, until your grace returns to me, and you speak to my heart.

Christ

I am here and I come to you because you called out to me. Your tears and the desire of your soul, your humility, and the contrition of your heart have attracted me and led me to you.

Disciple

And Lord, I called to you, wanting to enjoy your company. For love of you I am ready to renounce all things, because it was you who stirred me up to seek you. Be blessed, Lord, for granting this favor to your servant in your abundant mercy.

What more can I, your servant, say in your presence, except to profoundly humble myself before you, always aware that I am sinful and unworthy? Among all the wonders of heaven and earth, nothing can compare to you. All of your works are good, your judgments are true, and everything is ruled by your providence. Praise and glory be to you, O Wisdom of the Father! May my tongue, my soul, and all your creation praise and bless you.

— From Book 3, Chapter 21 (nos. 1–7)

XV

Remembering God's Innumerable Blessings

Disciple

Open my heart to your law, Lord, and teach me to walk in your commandments. Give me the grace to know your will and to remember reverently and diligently all your blessings, the general as well as the particular ones, so that I may always thank you adequately. I realize and I confess that I am incapable of properly thanking you. I am not worthy of the blessings you have granted me. While I consider your majesty, my spirit faints before your greatness.

All that we have in soul and body, all that we possess exteriorly and interiorly of the natural or supernatural order, are your gifts, which celebrate your generosity, mercy, and goodness. We have received all good things from you. Although some have received more, others less, all these gifts are yours. Without you not even the least of it would be possible. One who has received more cannot claim the glory, nor could such a one raise himself above others, nor insult those blessed with less as if anyone were greater or better than another. One will be worthy of greater things who attributes less to self, is more humble and devout in giving thanks, and esteems self to be totally unworthy of more gifts.

The one who receives fewer gifts should not be troubled by this, nor take it badly, nor envy one more richly blessed, but rather turn to you, praising your goodness for so generously, freely, and willingly bestowing your gifts without distinguishing among persons. Because all comes from you, you must be praised in all things. You know what should be given to each one. Why this person has less and the other more is not our business, but yours, for you know the merits of each one.

Therefore, Lord God, I consider it a great benefit to have few of those things that appear so valuable and are so highly praised; those things that cause some to see themselves impoverished and insignificant, and for lack of them to become disheartened and depressed. Rather I am consoled and very happy because you have chosen the poor, the humble and those of whom the world thinks little, as your friends and family.

Your apostles themselves, whom you made "princes in all the earth" (Ps 45:16), are witnesses of this. Nevertheless they lived in this world without complaint, so humble and so simple, without any malice or guile; "they rejoiced that they were considered worthy to suffer dishonor for the sake of the name" (Acts 5:41). They embraced with great love what the world abhors.

Nothing should give as much joy to those who love you and have experienced your blessings as having your will accomplished in them and sensing your pleasure in that. This makes it possible to be contented and consoled simply to be the least, while others strive to be the greatest, and to enjoy as much peace and contentment in the last place as could be felt in the first, and to willingly be despised and neglected, deprived of worldly recognition and reputation, as if they were the greatest and most respected persons in the world. All this because of the regard due to your will and your glory, which should console and please us more than any other possible benefits we have, or ever could receive.

— From Book 3, Chapter 22 (nos. 1–5)

XVI

Four Things That Bring Great Peace

Christ

My child, now I will teach you the way of peace and true freedom.

Disciple

Do as you say, Lord. This pleases me very much.

Christ

Try, my child, to do the will of another rather than your own. Always choose to have less rather than more. Always seek to take the last place, and to be subject to everyone. Always desire and pray that the will of God may be perfectly fulfilled in you. You will see that if you are disposed to do this you will find peace and serenity.

Disciple

Lord, your words have such perfection in them: few words, but so full of meaning and promise. If I would faithfully observe them, I would not be troubled so easily. I realize that whenever I find myself disquieted and disturbed, it is because I have strayed from your teachings.

Lord, you who can do all things and always love the good of my soul, increase your grace in me, so that I can put your words into practice and fulfill the work of my salvation.

A Prayer Against Evil Thoughts

O God, do not be far from me; O my God, make haste to help me (Ps 71:12), for all kinds of evil thoughts have risen up in me, and great fears trouble my spirit. How shall I pass through them unharmed? How shall I overcome them?

Christ

"I will go before you and level the mountains" (Isa 45:2). I will open the doors of the prison and reveal to you the most hidden secrets.

Disciple

Lord, do as you say so that in your presence all evil thoughts will flee. My only hope and consolation is to run to you in every trial, to confide in your help, to call on you wholeheartedly, and patiently await your consolation.

PRAYER TO OBTAIN ENLIGHTENMENT OF THE MIND

Enlighten me, good Jesus, with the brightness of the eternal light and chase from my heart all darkness. Restrain my many wandering thoughts and destroy the temptations that do me violence. Fight strongly for me and overcome the wicked beasts, that is, the alluring desires of my senses, so that peace may be obtained by your power and your praise may ring out from your holy temple (see Ps 122:7–8), that is, from my pure conscience.

Command the winds and storms, saying to the sea, "Be still!" (see Mk 4:39), and to the north wind, "Do not blow," and a great calm shall ensue.

"O send out your light and your truth" (Ps 43:3) to shine upon the earth. Enlighten me, because without you I am a sterile and desert land. Pour your grace from above, water my heart with heaven's dew, and send down the waters of devotion to irrigate the face of the earth, so that it may bring forth fruit that is good and perfect.

Lift up my mind, which is oppressed by the weight of sin, and lift up my desires toward heavenly things, so that, having tasted the sweetness of eternal happiness, I may regret thinking too much about worldly things.

Deliver me from the fleeting consolations of creatures, because created things can neither quiet nor fully satisfy my desires, nor can they console me. Join me to yourself with the indissoluble bond of love, for you alone can satisfy my love. Without you all other things are frivolous.

— From Book 3, Chapter 23 (nos. 1–10)

XVII

Calling Upon God and Blessing Him in Time of Trouble

Disciple

May your name be blessed forever, Lord, for you have been willing to allow that I should have this trial and suffering. I cannot escape it, so of necessity I come to you, so that you may help me and turn it to my good.

Lord, I am presently in tribulation and my heart is troubled; I am greatly afflicted by my present suffering. "Now my soul is troubled. And what should I say—'Father, save me from this hour'?" (Jn 12:27). No, this is the reason I am here, that you might be glorified when, in my humiliation, I am delivered by you. "Be pleased, O LORD, to deliver me" (Ps 40:13), for poor unfortunate one that I am, what can I do and where shall I go without you? Give me patience, Lord, even for this time. Help me, my God, and I will not fear, no matter how distressed I am.

And now, in the middle of all this, what shall I say? Lord, your will be done: perhaps I have deserved this affliction and this oppression. In any case, I must bear it until the storm passes and things get better. God, if you are willing I will endure it with patience, But your almighty hand is also able to remove this temptation from me and lessen its force as you have so often done in the past, O my God, my Mercy, so that I may not fall under it. The more difficult this is for me, the easier it is for your mighty arm to effect this change.

— From Book 3, Chapter 29 (nos. 1–2)

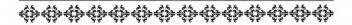

XVIII

On Asking God's Assistance and Confidently Regaining Grace

Christ

My child, "The LORD is good, a stronghold in a day of trouble" (Nahum 1:7). Come to me whenever you need help. The greatest hindrance to receiving consolation is your apparent reluctance to pray. Before you ask me for anything earnestly, you try to find other consolations, delighting yourself in so many external things. When it happens that nothing helps you out, you remember that I am the One who saves those who trust in me. Other than me you will find no power, nor profitable advice, nor lasting remedy.

Now that you have survived the storm and recovered your spirit, try to grow strong again in the light of my tender mercy. I am here to lend a healing hand, to offer abundant, overflowing help beyond measure.

Is anything difficult to me? Shall I be like one who promises and does not perform? Where is your faith? Stand firm and persevere. Be patient and have courage; consolation will come to you in due time.

Wait patiently for me and I will come and cure you. It is temptation that bothers you and a useless fear that strikes you with terror. What do you get from worry about what may come in the future, except a multitude of sorrows? "Today's trouble is enough for today" (Mt 6:34). It is vain and useless to feel grief or joy for future events that may never take place.

Although it is natural for us to be deceived by such worries, it is a sign of a weak soul easily drawn away by the suggestions of the enemy. For he does not care if it is true or not when he tricks and deceives you. It matters little whether he overcomes you with love of things present or fear of things to come. "Do not let your hearts be troubled, and do not let them be afraid" (Jn 14:27). Believe in me and confide in my mercy.

I am often closest to you when you think that I am far away. When you think that almost all is lost, it is often then that you are about to gain the greatest merit. All is not lost when something happens contrary to what you wanted. You must not judge according to how you feel at present, nor give yourself up easily to any trouble no matter where it comes from, nor imagine that all hope of deliverance is gone.

Do not think of yourself as completely forsaken, even if for a while I have sent you some tribulation, or taken some consolation away from you that you desire, for this is the road to the kingdom of heaven. Without a doubt it is more useful for you, and for the rest of my servants, that you be tried by adversity instead of having everything go according to your desires.

I know your hidden thoughts. I know that it is very necessary for your salvation that at times you should be left without any consolation. Otherwise you might become proud of your success and complacent about yourself, thinking that you are what you are not. What I have given, I can rightly take away and then give back again when I please.

When I give it to you, it is still mine. When I take it away again, I am not taking anything that is yours. "Every generous act of giving, with every perfect gift, is from above" (Jas 1:17). If I send you affliction or some adversity, do not grieve or be downhearted. I can quickly lift you up again and turn all your trouble into joy. However, I am to be praised when I deal with you in this way, for I am just.

If you are thinking correctly and consider things in truth, you should never be too downhearted or troubled by adversity. Instead you should rejoice and give thanks. Count it as a special joy that I do not spare you, but send you sorrow.

I said to my beloved disciples that "As the Father has loved me, so I have loved you" (Jn 15:9), and I certainly did not send them to temporal joys, but to great battles; not to honors, but to contempt; not to idleness, but to work; not to rest, but to "bear fruit with patient endurance" (Lk 8:15). Keep these words in mind, my child.

— From Book 3, Chapter 30 (nos. 1–6)

XIX

There Is No Security
from Temptation in This Life

Christ

If you seek rest in this life, how will you arrive at eternal rest? Do not concentrate on getting rest so much as on acquiring patience. Seek true peace not here on earth, but in heaven, not in other persons, not in any creatures, but only in God.

For the love of God you must willingly suffer all things, that is, work, sorrow, temptation, annoyance, anxiety, need, illness, injury, calumny, rebuke, humiliation, confusion, correction, and contempt. All of these gain virtue, try your good intention, and obtain for you the heavenly crown.

I will give an eternal reward for very short labor, infinite glory for passing confusion. Do you imagine that you can have spiritual consolation whenever you want it? My saints did not. They met with trouble, temptation, and great desolation. However, they endured all these with patience, confiding more in God than in themselves. They knew that "the sufferings of this present time are not worth comparing with the glory about to be revealed to us" (Rom 8:18).

Will you then immediately have what they hardly obtained even after many tears and much effort? "Wait for the LORD; be strong, and let your heart take courage: wait for the LORD! (Ps 27:14). Do not despair or give up, but offer both soul and body constantly for the glory of God.

I will reward you abundantly and be with you in all your trials.

— From Book 3, Chapter 35 (no. 1)

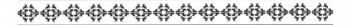

XX

We Should Deny Ourselves and Imitate Christ by the Cross

Christ

My child, you will be able to enter into me to the extent that you go out of yourself. As desiring nothing external brings peace, so does leaving yourself behind freely join you interiorly to God. I would like you to learn perfect self-renunciation according to my will, without contradiction or complaint. Follow me; "I am the way, and the truth, and the life" (Jn 14:6). Without the way there is no going; without the truth there is no knowing; without life there is no living. I am the Way that you must follow; the Truth that you must believe; the Life that you must hope for. I am the Way inviolable, the Truth infallible, and the Life interminable. I am the straightest Way, the sovereign Truth, the true Life, the blessed Life, and uncreated Life. If you continue in my way you will know the truth, and the truth shall make you free, and you will attain everlasting life.

"If you wish to enter into life, keep the commandments" (Mt 19:17). If you wish to know the truth, believe me. "If you wish to be perfect, go, sell your possessions" (Mt 19:21). If you wish to be my disciples, deny yourself. If you wish to have a blessed life, do not get lost in this present life. If you wish to be exalted in heaven, humble yourself in this world. If you wish to reign with me, carry the cross with me. No one but the servants of the cross find their way to the light and happiness of heaven.

Disciple

Lord Jesus, although your way is narrow and despised by the world, may I follow you despite the world's contempt. "A disciple is not above the teacher, nor a slave above the master" (Mt 10:24). Let me be trained on the example of your life, for there is my salvation and true sanctity. Whatever else I read or hear fails to refresh or delight me.

Christ

My child, now that you know these things and have read them all, blessed will you be if you carry them out. "They who have my commandments and keep them are those who love me; and those who love me will be loved by my Father, and I will love them and reveal myself to them"(Jn 14:21), and I will bring them to sit down with me in the kingdom of my Father.

Disciple

Lord Jesus, let everything be as you have promised, and let me merit it, too. I have received the cross from your hand. I will carry it even until my death because you have given it to me. I see that the life of a fervent person is a cross, but that cross is also the guide that leads to heaven. We have started out and may not go back, nor may we abandon it.

Take courage, friends. Let us go on together. Jesus will be with us. For him we have picked up the cross; for his sake let us continue on. He will help us as our Captain and our Forerunner. Our King who marches ahead of us will also fight for us. Let us follow him courageously. Let no one fear terrors. Let us prepare to die heroically in the battle; let us not disgrace ourselves by flying from the cross.

— From Book 3, Chapter 56 (nos. 1–6)

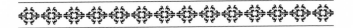

XXI

Christ Should Be Received
with Great Reverence

Disciple

Many go to different nations to visit the relics of the saints and marvel at their wonderful deeds. They contemplate their magnificent shrines and kiss their sacred bones enveloped in silk and gold. Yet you are present to me here on this altar, my God, the Saint of saints, the Creator of all and the Lord of angels.

People are often moved to see these things out of curiosity and a desire for novelty, so they obtain little fruit of amendment. This is even more so when persons run here and there without being moved by true contrition for their sins. But here, in the sacrament of the altar, you are entirely present, my God, the man Christ Jesus. Here we receive the fruit of salvation abundantly each time that we reverently and worthily receive you. We are not drawn to this sacrament lightly, out of curiosity or a desire to gratify our senses, but by a constant faith, a devout hope, and a pure charity.

O invisible God, Creator of the universe, how wonderfully you deal with us! You act so sweetly and so kindly toward us, your chosen, offering yourself to be received in this sacrament! This defies all human understanding and attracts to itself especially the hearts of the devout, and inflames their affection. Those truly faithful to you, who spend their entire lives trying to better themselves, often receive from this holy sacrament the great benefit of fervor and love of virtue.

Oh, the admirable and secret grace of this sacrament, known only to Christ's faithful, cannot be experienced by unbelievers or sinners. In this sacrament, spiritual grace is received; lost virtue is restored in the soul; and beauty marred by sin comes back again. Sometimes the grace received from the fullness of devotion is so great that not only the mind, but also the fragile body experiences an increase of strength.

Despite this, we must feel sorry about, and greatly lament, our lukewarmness and negligence because we do not go with greater fervor to receive Jesus Christ, in whom rests all the hope and merit of those who wish to be saved. He is our sanctification and our redemption. He is the consolation of pilgrims and the everlasting happiness of the saints. It is a cause of great sorrow that many disregard this saving mystery, which delights heaven and preserves the entire world. How blind and hardened the human heart, which values so little this ineffable gift, treating the sacrament with such indifference and receiving it out of habit.

For if this most holy sacrament were celebrated only in one place in the whole world and consecrated by only one priest, with how great a desire, do you think, would people wish to go to that place and to that priest of God, in order to see the divine mysteries celebrated?

Now, instead, there are many priests and Christ is offered up in many places, so that God's grace and love for us may appear so much the greater because this Holy Communion is so widely distributed throughout the world.

I thank you, good Jesus, eternal Shepherd, because you have willed to feed us poor exiles with your precious Body and Blood, and that you invite us to partake of these mysteries by words you yourself said, "Come to me, all you that are weary and are carrying heavy burdens, and I will give you rest" (Mt 11:28).

— From Book 4, Chapter 1 (nos. 9–13)

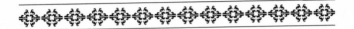

XXII

It Is Profitable
to Receive Communion Frequently

Disciple

Give yourself to me and that will be enough for me. Aside from you no consolation satisfies me. Without you I cannot live, and without receiving you I cannot exist. Therefore, I must approach you often and receive you in order to restore health to my soul. Otherwise if I were deprived of this heavenly food, I would faint on the way.

Most merciful Jesus, you once said this yourself when you were preaching to the people and healing various kinds of diseases: "I do not want to send them away hungry, for they might faint on the way" (Mt 15:32). Treat me this same way, you, who have left yourself in this sacrament for the consolation of the faithful. You are the sweet Nourishment of the soul. Whoever receives you worthily shall be a partaker and heir of eternal glory.

It is so necessary for me, who often falls into sin and who so quickly grows lax and faint, that by frequent prayers and confessions and by the Holy Communion of your Body, I may be reanimated, purified, and inflamed, so that I may not fail to keep my holy resolution.

"For the inclination of the human heart is evil from youth" (Gen 8:21), and if your heavenly medicine does not help us, we soon fall into worse things. Holy Communion will withdraw us from evil and comfort us in good.

For if I am often negligent and tepid now when I communicate or celebrate, what would happen if I did not receive this medicine and did not seek so great a help? Although I do not feel well prepared or disposed to celebrate every day, nevertheless I will try to receive the divine mysteries in the proper times, and participate in so great a grace. Contemplating you and being able to receive you with as much devotion as possible is our only consolation, so long as we live far away from you in this mortal body.

Your marvelous humility and compassion for us prompt you, Lord God, Creator and Life of every soul, to come to my poor soul and satisfy my hunger with your divinity and humanity! O happy mind and blessed soul, which merits to receive you with devotion, Lord God, and in receiving you, to be filled with spiritual happiness!

What a great Lord we entertain! What a beloved guest we bring into our house! What a sweet companion we receive! What a faithful friend we acquire! What a beautiful and noble spouse we embrace, to be loved beyond and above all things that we could love or desire! Let heaven and earth, with all their splendor, be silent in your presence, my sweet beloved, for whatever about them is worthy of praise or beautiful comes from you. They can never approach the splendor of your Name, you whose wisdom is incomprehensible.

— From Book 4, Chapter 3 (nos. 2–4)

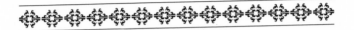

XXIII

Many Benefits Are Given to Those Who Receive You with Devotion

Disciple

Lord, in the simplicity of my heart, with a good and firm faith and in obedience to your command, I come to you full of hope and respect. I truly believe that you are present in the sacrament, as God and man. You desire that I receive you, united to you in love. So I beg your mercy, and I ask for the special grace to be totally consumed in you and overflowing with your love, never looking anywhere else for consolation.

This most revered and most worthy sacrament is the health of the soul and body. It is medicine for all spiritual ills, healing of our deep-rooted sins, guard on our passions. By it temptations are lessened or overcome, grace is abundantly infused, virtue is increased, faith is confirmed, hope is fortified, and charity is inflamed and increased.

O my God, the Defender of my soul, the Healer of human infirmity and the Giver of all interior consolations, in this sacrament you have given and continue to give many good things to your beloved who communicate devoutly. You are consolation in their trials. You lift them from the depths of dejection to the hope of your protection. You refresh and enlighten them with new grace, so that they, who before Communion felt anguished and without fervor, after having restored themselves with this heavenly food and drink, find themselves changed for the better.

In bestowing graces, you are pleased to deal this way with your faithful people so that they may truly acknowledge and openly experience how great is their weakness and how much greater is the bountiful grace they receive from you. For of themselves they are cold, arid, and lacking fervor, but by your mercy they obtain the grace to become fervent, zealous, and devout. In fact, who approaches the fountain of his mercy humbly and does not carry away a little of its sweetness; or standing by a great fire, does not derive from it a little warmth? You are a fountain that is ever full and overflowing, a fire that always burns and is never consumed....

Indeed, I labor by the sweat of my brow. My heart is in anguish and I am burdened by my sins. Temptations assail me. I am trapped by evil passions and oppressed. It seems there is no one to help me, no one to deliver and save me, but you, O Lord God, my Savior. I entrust myself and all that is mine to you. Guard me and lead me to eternal life. You have prepared your Body and Blood for my food and drink, now receive me to the praise and glory of your Name. Grant, O Lord, God of my salvation, that by participating often in your mystery, the fervor of my devotion may increase.

— From Book 4, Chapter 4 (nos. 2–3, 5)

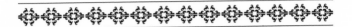

XXIV

On Christ's Self-Offering on the Cross and Our Self-Resignation

Christ

With my hands stretched out and my body naked upon the cross, I willingly offered myself to God my Father, for your sins. Nothing remained in me which was not taken up in sacrifice to the divine propitiation. As wholeheartedly as you can, you must willingly offer yourself to me daily in the Mass, as a pure and holy oblation, together with all your ability and affections. What more do I ask of you than that you try to fully give yourself over to me? Whatever you give me outside of yourself does not interest me because I do not seek your gift, I seek you.

What would it be for you, if you had everything except me? Whatever you give me matters not, if you do not give yourself to me. Offer yourself to me, giving your entire self for God, and your gift will be pleasing. I offered my whole self to the Father for you. I gave myself, body and blood for your food, so that I might be all yours and you might be all mine.

If you hold yourself back and will not spontaneously offer yourself to my will, your offering is not perfect, nor will our union be perfect. Therefore, all your actions must be preceded by a spontaneous offering of yourself into the hands of God, if you wish to gain freedom of spirit and my grace. Few are enlightened and interiorly free, because they do not know how to renounce themselves entirely.

My teaching remains unchanged: "None of you can become my disciple if you do not give up all your possessions" (Lk 14:33). If, therefore, you wish to be my disciple, offer yourself and all your affections to me.

— From Book 4, Chapter 8 (nos. 1–2)

XXV

A Devout Soul Should Desire Wholeheartedly to Be United to Christ in This Sacrament

Disciple

Truly you are my Beloved, "distinguished among ten thousand" (Song 5:10); in whom my soul is pleased to live all the days of her life. Truly you are the source of my peace. In you is supreme peace and true rest, and without you there is only labor, sorrow, and infinite misery.

In truth you are the hidden God. You speak to the humble and the simple and have nothing to do with the wicked. How dear to us is your spirit, Lord, for you show your love to your children by feeding us with that sweet Bread which comes down from heaven! "For what other great nation has a god so near to it as the LORD our God is whenever we call to him?" (Deut 4:7). You give yourself to us to eat and taste, as our daily comfort, and to lift our hearts to heaven.

For what other people is as blessed as the Christian people? Or who under heaven is as beloved as a devout soul, to whom God comes and feeds with his glorious flesh? O ineffable grace! O admirable condescension! O immense love, so singularly bestowed upon us!

"What shall I return to the LORD for all his bounty to me?" (Ps 116:12), and for so great a love? There is nothing I can give him that will be more acceptable than to give my heart totally and to unite my heart intimately to my God. Then, when my heart is perfectly united to God, all within me will rejoice exceedingly.

He will say to me: If you want to be with me, then I want to be with you. And I will answer: Yes, Lord, remain with me, because I sincerely want to be with you. This is my only desire, that my heart be united to you.

— From Book 4, Chapter 13 (nos. 2–3)

XXVI

The Ardent Desire
of Some Devout Persons
to Receive the Body of Christ

Disciple

"O how abundant is your goodness that you have laid up for those who fear you" (Ps 31:19). When I remember those devout persons who approach your sacrament with great fervor and affection, I become confused and blush with shame to present myself at your altar and to the table of Holy Communion because I am so tepid and cold.

Why do I remain so dry, with no affection? Why am I not completely enflamed in your presence, O my God? Why am I not strongly attracted and moved, as were so many devout persons, whose hearts were so filled with love that they could not contain their tears in their immense desire for Holy Communion?

But body and soul they longed for you, my God, the living Fountain. They did not know how to moderate or satisfy their hunger in any other way than by receiving your Body joyously with a lively spiritual desire.

The ardent faith of these persons serves as an argument to prove your sacred presence! Truly they know their Lord in the breaking of the bread, and their hearts burn strongly within them for love of Jesus who walks with them. Such love and devotion is often far from me.

Be merciful to me, good, sweet, and gracious Jesus. Grant your poor beggar at least occasionally a bit of the gracious sentiment of your love in Holy Communion, so that my faith may be strengthened, my hope in your goodness increased, and my charity, once perfected, fanned into flame. Having tasted heaven's manna may I never faint.

How powerful your mercy, which gives me the grace I desire and kindly visits me with an increased spirit of fervor whenever it pleases you. In fact, although at present I do not burn with this great desire, as do your most devoted, nevertheless, I am confident that in your grace you will nourish this desire that I have to be numbered among the company of your fervent lovers.

— From Book 4, Chapter 14 (nos. 1–3)

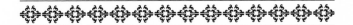

XXVII

The Grace of Devotion Acquired by Humility and Self-Denial

Christ

You must seek the grace of devotion constantly, ask for it with ardent desire, wait for it with patience and confidence, receive it with gratitude, conserve it with humility, use it with diligence, and leave to God the time and the manner of heavenly visitation, until it pleases him to come to you.

Before everything else, humble yourself when you feel little or no interior devotion; but do not become too dejected, nor grieve inordinately. In one short moment

God often gives what he has denied for a long time. At the end of prayer he sometimes gives that which in the beginning he did not give.

If grace were always immediately granted, and were at hand whenever desired, human weakness would be unable to bear it. However, the grace of devotion must be awaited with firm hope and with humble patience. When it is not given to you, or when it is secretly taken away, blame yourself and your sins. Sometimes a little thing hinders grace and makes it withdraw from you, if that which deprives you of so great a good can be called little and not great. But if you remove this small or great thing, and perfectly overcome it, you shall receive what you asked for.

For as soon as you have consecrated yourself with all your heart to God, and have not sought this or that thing for your own pleasure, but wholly leaned upon him, you will immediately find yourself recollected and at peace. Nothing will give you such joy or please you as much as the good pleasure of God's will.

Whoever, therefore, with simplicity of heart lift their intentions to God, purifying themselves from all disordered attractions or inordinate aversion for any creature, shall be fit to receive grace and worthy of the gift of devotion.

The Lord gives his blessing where he finds vessels empty. The more perfectly you renounce the things of the world, and the more you die to yourself by your humility, the more quickly grace will come to you. It will enter the heart more abundantly, and lift to greater heights the heart that is free and unattached.

"Then you shall see and be radiant; your heart shall thrill and rejoice" (Isa 60:5). The Lord's hand is with you because you have placed yourself into his hands completely and forever. In this way you are blessed when you seek God wholeheartedly, not neglecting your own soul. In receiving the Holy Eucharist, you merit the extraordinary grace of union with God not by paying attention to your own devotion and consolation, but by placing the honor and glory of God above your own concern.

— From Book 4, Chapter 15 (nos. 1–4)

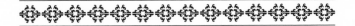

XXVIII

We Must Manifest Our Necessities to Christ and Ask His Grace

Disciple

Sweet and loving Lord, whom I now desire to receive devoutly, you know my weakness and the troubles I am enduring, how many evils and vices I am immersed in, and how often I am oppressed, tempted, troubled, and stained by sin. To you I come to be cured; I implore your consolation and help. I confide in you because you know all things. Everything in me is known to you, and you alone can perfectly console and help me. You know the good I stand most in need of and how poor I am in virtues.

Behold, I stand before you, poor and naked, asking your grace and imploring your mercy. Feed your hungry beggar, heat my coldness with the fire of your love, enlighten my blindness with the splendor of your presence. Turn all earthly things into bitterness for me, all burdensome and contrary things into patient forbearance, and all created things into things of little importance that will someday end.

Uplift my heart to you in heaven, and do not permit me to wander aimlessly over the earth. From now on and forever, may you alone be sweet to me; because you alone are my food and my drink, my love and my joy, my sweetness and my every good.

— From Book 4, Chapter 16 (nos. 1–2)

Sources

à Kempis, Thomas. *De Imitatione Christi*. http://www.thelatinlibrary.com/kempis.html.

———. *The Imitation of Christ*. Boston: St. Paul Editions, 1962.

Pauline
BOOKS & MEDIA

The Daughters of St. Paul operate book and media centers at the following addresses. Visit, call, or write the one nearest you today, or find us on the World Wide Web, www.pauline.org.

CALIFORNIA

3908 Sepulveda Blvd, Culver City, CA 90230 — 310-397-8676
2650 Broadway Street, Redwood City, CA 94063 — 650-369-4230
5945 Balboa Avenue, San Diego, CA 92111 — 858-565-9181

FLORIDA

145 S.W. 107th Avenue, Miami, FL 33174 — 305-559-6715

HAWAII

1143 Bishop Street, Honolulu, HI 96813 — 808-521-2731
Neighbor Islands call: — 866-521-2731

ILLINOIS

172 North Michigan Avenue, Chicago, IL 60601 — 312-346-4228

LOUISIANA

4403 Veterans Memorial Blvd, Metairie, LA 70006 — 504-887-7631

MASSACHUSETTS

885 Providence Hwy, Dedham, MA 02026 — 781-326-5385

MISSOURI

9804 Watson Road, St. Louis, MO 63126 — 314-965-3512

NEW YORK

64 W. 38th Street, New York, NY 10018 — 212-754-1110

PENNSYLVANIA

Philadelphia—relocating — 215-676-9494

SOUTH CAROLINA

243 King Street, Charleston, SC 29401 — 843-577-0175

VIRGINIA

1025 King Street, Alexandria, VA 22314 — 703-549-3806

CANADA

3022 Dufferin Street, Toronto, ON M6B 3T5 — 416-781-9131

¡También somos su fuente para libros,
videos y música en español!